Prayer Changes Things

Curing Timid Piety

P. Andrew Sandlin

ISBN: 13: 978-1984995056
ISBN-10: 1984995057

To Cornerstone Bible Church, Scotts Valley, California

Together, we learned to pray — and get answers.

CONTENTS

PREFACE

The Bible spills over with truth about prayer. If you don't believe this, I invite you to access a topical Bible or other book that categorizes the Bible's teaching by topic and investigate "prayer." You might be surprised by what you find. The mere preponderance of prayer suggests it is a matter to which we Christians should devote serious attention — more serious attention than we generally do.[1]

I was reared in a prayer-drenched family. My parents prayed frequently and fervently, and God answered them. My late mother's short comments I cite at the end of chapter 2 testify to this fact. As I developed intense theological and other intellectual interests in my late teens, my ardor for prayer cooled. About ten years ago, however, God in his good providence used one of his choice souls to lay in my hands a book I'd known about for a quarter century but had never

---

[1] Theologians sometimes criticize such "topical textbooks" for decontextualizing the topics and for being insensitive to the progress of redemptive history (where in God's historical plan does this topic unfold, and how and why?). While legitimate criticisms, there can be no doubt that a great advantage of topical textbooks is that they acquaint the reader with the sheer weight of biblical evidence on a topic. In the case of prayer, you might miss that weight without observing it in consolidation. In short, the Bible teaches a lot more about prayer than you might think — certainly a lot more than Christians today usually do

fully read: E. M. Bounds' *The Weapon of Prayer*. That utterly biblical, faith-drenched book by arguably the greatest writer on prayer since the apostle Paul completely revived and reoriented my prayer life and theology. I read Bounds' entire works on prayer. In fact, I'm now reading through that work for the fourth time, and I hope to re-read it another twenty-five times before I die. I've read other great books on prayer, including the fascinating *The Soul of Prayer* by P. T. Forsyth. None quite compares to Bounds. This present booklet is in many ways just a restatement and updating of their irrefutable arguments and buoying exhortations. It is nothing close to a comprehensive treatment of the issue of prayer, or even a summary of the leading issues. It simply tackles what are in my view particularly pertinent themes and problems.

I didn't write the main body with theologians and other scholars in mind. However, I've included in the footnotes both my sources and some technical theological matters that my view both assumes and creates.

This booklet includes repetition because I've addressed some of the same issues from different angles and in different contexts. The first three chapters have a conversational and exhortative tone because they were originally delivered as messages to Cornerstone Bible Church (Scotts Valley, California) or to the Wilberforce Academy (Cambridge, England). Chapter 4 appears here for the first time.

I should also mention that there is no more important book or booklet that I have ever written or likely will ever write.

CHAPTER 1

PRAYER CHANGES THINGS

Introduction

If you've ever visited Christian bookstores, you likely have seen bracelets or plaques or bumper stickers with the statement, "Prayer Changes Things." For years I thought that statement was trite. After all, lots of these bookstore statements are trite: "God is my copilot," "Christians aren't perfect, just forgiven," "Honk if you love Jesus." But over the years, the more I pondered "Prayer changes things" the more I've come to believe that it is true, and not only true, but precisely and powerfully true in a sense we Christians do not often consider. The culprit is that we misunderstand prayer.

Prayer is more than communion

We are called to commune with God. We worship him. We think about him, we ponder who he is and what he has done in the world. We stand in awe of the sovereign, triune God.

But this is not the same thing as prayer. Almost all prayer in the Bible is petitionary. By that I mean: in prayer, we ask God to do things in the earth. More importantly, we ask God to *change* things. Prayer actually is asking God to change the status quo. Things are a certain way — our hearts are cold, or a relative has cancer, or we lack money for our bills, or our children are drifting from the Lord, or we need direction for a decision, whatever — and we ask God to change the way things are. In other words, we're not satisfied with the status quo. That is a legitimate godly dissatisfaction, and we must not shrink from this truth. Ungodly dissatisfaction is when God does good things for us (sometimes even good things we perceive as not good), and we don't accept what he's done. But godly dissatisfaction is when things are out of kilter, displeasing or harming us or impeding the gospel or the kingdom of God, and we ask God to change them. There's nothing illegitimate about that kind of dissatisfaction. We need more of it, in fact.

Some people seem to have the idea that if we ask God for things, if we petition God, that's somehow self-centered or unspiritual. Only if we're worshiping God or telling him how great he is are we truly glorifying him. This is a very mistaken, and possibly even a spiritually fatal, idea.

In addressing the Lord's Prayer, the commentator Matthew Henry notes that the devout Jews of Jesus' time would often pray by telling God how great he is.[1] This is a necessary, fundamental and entirely appropriate way of approaching him. But Henry writes that when Jesus taught his disciples to pray, he told him to utter petitions. In other words, he told them to ask his Father for things. When we ask God for things, we are not somehow less spiritual than when we

---

[1] Matthew Henry, *Commentary on the Whole Bible*, at Luke 11, http://www.biblestudytools.com/commentaries/matthew-henry-complete/luke/11.html, accessed January 22, 2018.

tell God how great he is. Answered prayer is greatly more God-honoring than unanswered prayer.

Answered prayer glorifies God

Why is this? For one thing, when we pray, and when God answers prayer, he increases our faith, and he shows the world his great might and power. Let's take one petition in the Lord's Prayer: thy kingdom come, thy will be done, on earth as it is in heaven. When God answers that prayer, when people turn to Jesus Christ for salvation, when they start living godly lives, when artists and businessmen and politicians start doing God's will, God glorifies himself. Unbelievers look around and say, "This God must be some kind of God to do all of this when his followers ask him. Nobody *I* ask has ever been able to do something so massive!" In other words, God gets the glory when we pray and when he answers our prayers. And know this: God loves to get the glory (2 Cor. 10:17). He deserves to get the glory.

Prayer changes things. When we pray, we're asking God to change things. And when he answers our prayer, he does change things. This brings us to a most telling fact that we don't often consider: if we are perfectly willing always to accept the way things are as God's unchangeable will, we will never be great people of prayer. Great prayer warriors are people who want things to change. They don't accept the status quo, the present circumstances. Prayer changes things. Prayer changes circumstances. Prayer changes people. And prayer changes God.

I want to demonstrate these assertions most graphically in a passage from the life of Elijah the prophet, 1 Kings 17:17–24. I could've selected hundreds of passages in the Bible (yes, literally hundreds), but this one is especially powerful. It relates a striking account about the widow with whom Elijah lodged and for whom God provided during the great, God-unleashed drought as judgment during the reign of apostate King Ahab:

Now it happened after these things that the son of the woman who owned the house became sick. And his sickness was so serious that there was no breath left in him. So she said to Elijah, "What have I to do with you, O man of God? Have you come to me to bring my sin to remembrance, and to kill my son?" And he said to her, "Give me your son." So he took him out of her arms and carried him to the upper room where he was staying, and laid him on his own bed. Then he cried out to the Lord and said, "O Lord my God, have You also brought tragedy on the widow with whom I lodge, by killing her son?" And he stretched himself out on the child three times, and cried out to the Lord and said, "O Lord my God, I pray, let this child's soul come back to him." Then the Lord heard the voice of Elijah; and the soul of the child came back to him, and he revived. And Elijah took the child and brought him down from the upper room into the house, and gave him to his mother. And Elijah said, "See, your son lives!" Then the woman said to Elijah, "Now by this I know that you are a man of God, and that the word of the Lord in your mouth is the truth."

Prayer Changes Circumstances

Note, first, that prayer changes *circumstances*. God had sent a great drought on Israel because Elijah had prayed for it. Ahab was the king, and he and his wife Jezebel were apostates and idolaters. Elijah was God's prophet, and he'd read God's law, which threatens that if God's people apostatize, he will shut up the heavens so that they will not send rain (Dt. 28:23–24). In other words, Elijah prayed, and he declared God's actions according to God's revealed will.

Think about this fact. Elijah didn't need to ponder what the will of God was. He knew what the will of God was. If God's people turn away from him, God promised to punish them in a very specific way. Elijah prayed that God would do just that. Elijah prayed that

God would act according to his word. That's always a safe prayer to pray: praying the biblically revealed will of God.

As result of the drought, there was little food and water. God led Elijah to the home of the widow and her son, and God miraculously provided for her so that she could provide for Elijah. After awhile, this faithful woman's son got sick and died, and you can imagine how grieved she was and, in fact, how resentful she was of Elijah, whom God had sent to invade her home (see v. 18). Elijah too was deeply shaken. Why would God unleash this tragedy?

Predestinarian prayers

Now, I draw your attention to a most remarkable fact. In observing this child's death, and in seeing the mother's grief, Elijah did not pray a "predestinarian prayer." He didn't pray, "Lord, you've allowed this precious child to die, and obviously that's your will, so we accept your will." Nor did he encourage the mother simply to accept her son's death as God's will. Elijah apparently did not believe that it would be pious, that it would be God-honoring, to allow the child to remain dead. Elijah refused the accept the status quo as the will of God.

Elijah knew that prayer changes things. To elaborate on an assertion above: if you constantly accept the status quo as God's predestined will (his eternal decrees), you cannot be a mighty man or woman of prayer. Too often we are so worried about violating the secret decrees of God that we turn our backs on the revealed word of God.

Are we better parents than God?

God is a powerful, prayer-hearing God, and he longs as a heavenly Father to do good things for his people. The Bible teaches this very plainly (Mt. 7:11). Yes, sometimes God allows "bad things to happen to good people" (Job), but that's not the way he operates most of the time. He is a loving, heavenly Father to his children, and just as you want to do good things for your children, so he wants to do good things for his children. Unless you believe that you are a better parent than God is?

So let's be very careful about using God's secret councils as an excuse not to petition God. They are called God's *secret* councils for a reason. We can't know them. Let's pray according to what we do know, and not according to what we do not know. And we do know that God is a loving, kind, Father who wishes to delight his children.

Prayer changes circumstances, and it changed this widow's circumstances.

Prayer Changes People

Second, prayer changes people. This child was dead. Elijah prayed, and God raised him from the dead. This is not an example of a modern "healing ministry." You might know about a large charismatic church in Redding, California that specializes in alleged public resurrections. There's a huge amount of weirdness and goofiness and theological error surrounding this ministry, but one thing I want to point out is that when Elijah raised this child from the dead, there was no public fanfare. There wasn't any fanfare at all — the prayer wasn't answered in public. In other words, this wasn't an example of an "answered prayer party." These "healing ministries" that bring in hundreds or thousands of spectators and bring glory to man and bring money into the coffers are a prostitution of the biblical teaching about prayer. When God used Elijah to raise this boy, three people knew. Only three people and God needed to know.

Prayer changes people. God gives us volition and choice, and he doesn't turn us into robots or machines. We are created in God's image, and that image includes volition. But God can work in our and in other people's lives in such a way as to change us. This means that we can pray that God changes people. And we should.

This is why Paul tells Timothy (1 Tim. 2:2) to teach his flock that they should pray for their political leaders, so that the people of

God can live a quiet and peaceful life. In other words, we should pray that God changes the hearts of political leaders so that they leave the church and God's people alone to do God's work.

God is intentionally vulnerable to prayer

There are several times in the Bible (see, for example, Jer. 14:11) where God tells his prophets not to pray for his people. In other words, they had turned their back on God so much, and he didn't want his prophets trying to persuade him not to send judgment. This means that God recognizes that prayer to him for people can be very effective. God knows that his own heart is vulnerable to the persevering prayer of his saints. God wants to answer prayer. God *wants* to be persuaded to avert his wrath.

Prayer changes people. I don't mean by that that if we pray, the act of prayer will change *us*. Of course, that's true. When we pour out our hearts to God, we get much closer to him, by the very nature of prayer itself. Our minds and hearts are riveted to spiritual things. We gradually lose our worldliness. God changes people who pray.

I mean something else. I mean that we should pray for God to change people, and he will change them. Just as God raised this child in answer to Elijah's prayer, so he can and will raise sinners to eternal life because of our prayer. The question for us is: do we pray for God to save sinners? And if not, why not?

If we answer, "Well, we don't know if they are one of the elect," we give the wrong answer. All of God's chosen will be in the fold in the final day, but he uses prayer to get them there. God doesn't only elect men; he elects means. And one of those means is prayer.[2]

---

[2] I apply to prayer the reasoning Norman Shepherd employs in *The Call of Grace* (Phillipsburg, New Jersey: P & R Publishing, 2000), 67–105. Shepherd, whose book is subtitled *How the Covenant Illuminates Salvation and Evangelism*, argues that the Great Commission, election, and regeneration should be understood from the standpoint not of God's eternal decrees but of the covenant, that is, God's dealings

If our spouse or children or friends are walking away from the Lord, let's pray that God unleashes his bloodhounds to find them and bring them back. They bear the mark of baptism. That's the mark of discipleship. That means they've been given to the Lord.[3] They have been given to him, so let's pray that he goes and gets them. This isn't rocket science. This is godly prayer.

If our brothers and sisters are sick, we need to pray that God heals them. This isn't merely a good idea. This is what the Bible demands (Jas. 5:13–16). Think of that fact. God didn't say that prayer for healing is a wonderful privilege, if only we choose to exercise it. He says that if someone is sick, we need to pray that God heals them, and, in fact, they should call for the elders to anoint them and pray over them.

Yes, there are certain specific illnesses that are in God's will (2 Tim. 4:20). But in many, many cases, God sends illnesses so that we will pray and exercise faith and be healed and bring glory to God (Jn. 11:4). Physical healing no less than spiritual healing brings glory to God.

In other words, like Elijah, when someone is sick, even to the point of death, we shouldn't merely accept the status quo.

Why? Because prayer changes people.

Prayer Changes God

Finally, prayer changes God. This statement may not ring true in our ears. The Bible says plainly that God does not change (Mal. 3:6). Jesus Christ is the same yesterday, today, and forever (Heb. 13:8). Obviously, there is some sense in which God does not change.

---

in history anchored in his loving, binding, bilateral relationship with humanity. I could have titled this booklet *Covenant Prayer*. Covenant prayer is oriented to God's covenant promises in his word and not in our consideration or interpretation of his eternal decrees.

[3] Andrew Murray, *How to Raise Your Children for Christ* (Minneapolis: Bethany House, 1975), 30–43.

But we know that in another sense, he does change. Again and again the Bible says that God repents, or relents, or changes his mind (Gen. 6:6; Ex. 32:14; Dt. 32:36; Jer. 42:10).[4] This isn't a contradiction, and it's not hard to reconcile this apparent (but only apparent) contradiction.[5]

God's character doesn't change. He's always loving, just, holy, kind, and long suffering. God isn't capricious. God isn't flighty. God cannot be evil. He cannot be unrighteous. He cannot be unloving. His nature cannot change.

But his stated purposes can change, and they do change.[6] One of the most powerful proofs of this is Genesis 6, where we read that God looked on the earth in Noah's time, and he was grieved that he had created humanity. He was excited to have created man, and it grieved him that man had raced into depravity. He was sad that he had even created man in the first place.

In the book of Jonah we read that God says that within a few weeks, he'll completely destroy Nineveh for their depravity (1:2; 3:1–4). He didn't put any qualifications on that warning. He didn't say, "If you repent, I won't judge you." But they did repent, and God didn't destroy them.

God says he's going to do something, and then people pour out their hearts before God, and then he changes his mind. This happens again and again in the Bible, so many times, in fact, that we might want to say that it's *in God's nature* to change his mind when his people, and even sincere, humble sinners, pour out their souls to him. God delights to make himself open to change in the face of the heartfelt prayer.

---

[4] I'll elaborate in chapter 4.

[5] Carl F. H. Henry, *God, Revelation and Authority* (Waco, Texas: Word, 1983), 6:52–75.

[6] John M. Frame, *The Doctrine of God* (Phillipsburg, New Jersey: P & R Publishing, 2002), 561–566.

A great example is in our text. We read that twice Elijah "cried" to the Lord (vv. 20, 21). This means that he spoke emotionally, in a very loud voice. This is just the opposite of a "quiet-time" prayer. And we read in verse 22 that the Lord listened to or heard this loud, passionate prayer.

This verse implies something very important. God was set on the path to take the widow's son in death, and he did take him. That was his implied purpose. Elijah plainly says that this was God's purpose. But his great emotional plea turned God around. God changed what he had planned to do. Elijah prayed, and his prayer changed God.

Audacity in prayer

The Bible is quite clear that prayer changes God. If this is true, then we should be much more audacious in prayer than we are. We read in Exodus 32 about how Israel turned to idolatry and fornication when Moses was on Sinai receiving from God his law. God told Moses that he was going to destroy the entire nation and then he said something very interesting. He said to Moses, "Leave me alone" (v. 10). God knew that Moses was in the habit of "disturbing" him in prayer. God would say, "I'm going to do this," and Moses would say, "I beg you, God, don't do that," and God would change his mind.

To repeat: God's stated purposes can be changed if we pour out our hearts in prayer. This is another way of saying that God has made himself vulnerable and susceptible to man's pleading.

Therefore, when something bad has happened, or when someone has committed some terrible sin, don't just sit and wait for God's judgment. Get on your knees and beg God to avert his judgment and to lead them to repentance. God will never break his promises to us, but God is eager to change his declared purposes of judgment (and on other matters) if we pour out our hearts before him.

Do not think that your prayer cannot affect God. Do not think that God is not emotional about and vulnerable to his people. He gets furious at them when they turn their back on him, and he delights in them when they love and trust him and repent and obey. Therefore, appeal to God's mercy and honor and even his reputation (Ex. 32:11–14) when you pray.

Conclusion

Prayer changes circumstances. Prayer changes people. And prayer changes God.

If this is true, and it is, we should pray more, we should pray more often, we should pray more fervently, we should pray more confidently, and we should never settle for the status quo, because the whole point of prayer is for God to change the status quo.

CHAPTER 2

PRAY BIG, EXPECT BIG

Introduction

I t's genuinely remarkable how many prayers we find in the Bible and how many teachings about prayer we find in the Bible. The Bible is simply full of prayer.[1] If we took time actually to study the topic of prayer, we'd discover that it pervades the word of God. It's not a secondary topic; it's a major topic.

This is why prayerlessness in the church is so counterintuitive — and, I believe, sinister and satanic. After all, if our prayer moves God to change the status quo, revealing his mighty power and

---

[1] Herbert Lockyer, *All the Prayers of the Bible* (Grand Rapids: Zondervan, 1959).

advancing his kingdom, Satan has a vested interest in the prayerlessness of Christians.

Prayer is a basic but powerful part of Christian living. The Bible doesn't envision that we can live as a Christian without living a life of prayer. The church that does not major on prayer is not acting as a Christian church. The church not routinely getting prayers answered is not a normal Christian church. If you don't believe this, I simply ask you to read the book of Acts. The primitive church prayed, and that church routinely got answers to prayer. In short: if we're not praying, and we're not getting answers to prayer, there's something terribly wrong.

John 4:46–54 constitutes a tender, compelling account of one of Jesus' signs. It's an example of daring prayer.

> So Jesus came again to Cana of Galilee where He had made the water wine. And there was a certain nobleman whose son was sick at Capernaum. When he heard that Jesus had come out of Judea into Galilee, he went to Him and implored Him to come down and heal his son, for he was at the point of death. Then Jesus said to him, "Unless you people see signs and wonders, you will by no means believe." The nobleman said to Him, "Sir, come down before my child dies!" Jesus said to him, "Go your way; your son lives." So the man believed the word that Jesus spoke to him, and he went his way. And as he was now going down, his servants met him and told him, saying, "Your son lives!" Then he inquired of them the hour when he got better. And they said to him, "Yesterday at the seventh hour the fever left him." So the father knew that it was at the same hour in which Jesus said to him, "Your son lives." And he himself believed, and his whole household. This again is the second sign Jesus did when He had come out of Judea into Galilee.

I want us to draw important truths from this account and other biblical texts, and I want those truths to change how we pray.

Big Faith Does Not Annoy God

First, *our Lord is never miffed by daring prayers.* Never in the Bible do we find an example of Jehovah in the Old Testament or Jesus in the New Testament complaining that people ask God to do too much for them. On the contrary: God continually chides his people because they lack faith. Big, bold, daring prayers do not upset God. Little, anorexic, unbelieving prayers upset God.

In John 4 we read that a nobleman's son had suffered a near-fatal fever. He'd heard that the rabbi from Nazareth was healing the sick. So he approached Jesus and begged him to heal his son. One notable facet of this account is that Jesus didn't need to be present to miraculously heal. Imagine in a similar case our asking a physician to operate on a sick relative without being present. The nobleman had enough faith simply to trust the very word of Jesus.

Jesus said, "Go; your son will live." And then we read: "The man believed the word that Jesus spoke to him and went on his way."

This is simple, daring faith. The nobleman's faith was rewarded. As he was returning home, his servants met him and informed him that his son was recovering. "When did his fever start dropping?" he asked. The answer: the exact hour that Jesus said, "Go; your son will live."

God delights to answer big, daring prayers. I'm not implying that he's not interested in prayers for small, ordinary problems. Of course, he is. But he relishes great, visionary faith from his children. Earthly fathers delight when their children exercise great confidence in them. Can you imagine how the heavenly Father feels when his children have faith that he can do anything for them?

It's tragic how much faith we often lack. A couple of years ago I was talking to a dear friend on the East Coast. He had recently attended a church, of all things most conservative, which was praying that one of its ladies wouldn't suffer too much from her chemotherapy. They didn't pray that God would heal her of cancer, mind you, but that he would give her relief from her treatment. Apparently God is strong enough to relieve pain but not strong enough to heal disease. This is not a prayer of great faith, if I may say so.

In 2 Kings 13:14–19 we read the last recorded event of the life of the prophet Elisha, Elijah's successor. Apostate Israelite king Joash visited the prophet, saddened by his approaching death but also anxious at the impending attack of the Syrian army on Israel:

> Elisha had become sick with the illness of which he would die. Then Joash the king of Israel came down to him, and wept over his face, and said, "O my father, my father, the chariots of Israel and their horsemen!"

> And Elisha said to him, "Take a bow and some arrows." So he took himself a bow and some arrows. Then he said to the king of Israel, "Put your hand on the bow." So he put his hand on it, and Elisha put his hands on the king's hands. And he said, "Open the east window"; and he opened it. Then Elisha said, "Shoot"; and he shot. And he said, "The arrow of the Lord's deliverance and the arrow of deliverance from Syria; for you must strike the Syrians at Aphek till you have destroyed them." Then he said, "Take the arrows"; so he took them. And he said to the king of Israel, "Strike the ground"; so he struck three times, and stopped. And the man of God was angry with him, and said, "You should have struck five or six times; then you would have struck Syria till you had destroyed it! But now you will strike Syria only three times."

Elisha was angry at Joash's lack of faith. Elisha had implied that the extent of Israelite military victory was contingent on how many times Joash struck arrows on the ground. He had faith only for a paltry victory, not a comprehensive victory.

Again and again our Lord chided his disciples for their small faith (Mt. 6:30; 8:26; 16:8; Lk. 12:28). He never rebuked them for exercising too large a faith, of asking too much of him.[2]

God's Prescriptive Will or Decretive Will?

Second, *daring prayers should not consider God's secret, eternal counsels.* By this I mean, God's predestined will for human history. The Bible certainly teaches that God has a plan for human history, and that his plan will be accomplished (Is. 14:24–27; 46:8–10), but it is noteworthy the Bible has almost nothing to say about considering that plan when we are making requests of God. In this way, our prayers today are starkly different from the prayers of the saints in the Bible.

We pray, "God, *if it's your will*, please give us a child." Hannah prays, "Lord, please give me a child." And God gives her Samuel (1 Sam. 1).

We pray, "Jesus, *if it's in your Father's plan*, please heal us of this sickness." The disciples prayed, "Lord, please put your hand on this deaf and dumb man so that he can be healed" (Mk. 7:31–37). And Jesus healed him.

We pray, "Lord, *if it's part of your eternal will*, please send revival to your people and to our nation." Jehovah says,

> "When I shut up heaven and there is no rain, or command the locusts to devour the land, or send pestilence among My people, if My people who are called by My name will humble themselves, and pray and seek My face, and turn from their wicked ways,

---

[2] He did not answer the request of James and John's mother for them to sit next to him in the kingdom, but this was because the Father had not authorized the Son to grant that request (Mt. 20:20–28)

then I will hear from heaven, and will forgive their sin and heal their land." (2 Chr. 7:13–14)

My point is simple: we have almost no examples in the Bible of God's people who limit their prayers by pondering his secret councils. God's people rightly believe in his eternal will. We take great comfort in his will. But when we pray, we pray according to his revealed will in the Bible. We don't know the specifics of God's secret will. That's why it's secret. But God's will in the Bible is not secret; it's revealed. One thing we do know about God from his revealed will is that his secret will isn't accomplished by his producing world history as a full-length feature film and then kicking back and watching the movie he made. He's actively involved accomplishing his will by constantly interacting with man, created in his image — loving, commanding, rewarding, punishing, wooing, judging — in response to man's actions. This is the God revealed in the Bible.

We know what God's revealed will is. It's expressed in his word for all to read. And so we pray according to that revealed will.

This does not mean that God answers every prayer. No father gives his children everything they want; he would not be a faithful father if he did. God didn't answer Paul's prayer to remove the thorn of his flesh (2 Cor. 12:7–9). But he wants to do good things for his children, and most of the time he answers our prayers offered in faith. Is our heavenly Father less caring about our needs and desires than our earthly father (Mt. 7:7–11)?

Grant Osborne is right: "God is sovereign and can say 'no [to our prayer],' but we should not expect God to reject our requests."[3] Of course, God can say no, because God knows what's best. But just as we love to please our children whom we love, so God loves to please his children whom he loves. If we don't understand this tender

---

[3] Grant R. Osborne, "Moving Forward on our Knees: Corporate Prayer in the New Testament," *Journal of the Evangelical Theological Society* 53, 2 (June 2010): 255.

fact, we have missed something very crucial about prayer — and God.

And this is why is when we read the Bible, we can come up with some amazing statistics. Even apart from the Psalms, which are full of prayers, "[T]he Bible records no fewer than 650 definite prayers, of which no less than 450 have recorded answers."[4] That's a fascinating proportion. Probably more than 450 of the prayers in the Bible were answered. Still, that's almost 70% of answered prayers that we know of. God doesn't always answer our prayers, but he answers many more prayers than if we did not pray.

We must face that fact squarely: Had this nobleman not come to Jesus and begged for the healing of his son, we have no reason to believe his son would have been healed. It's futile for us to ask, "But what is the predestined will of God? Wouldn't God have healed him anyway if he had been predestined to be healed?" That answer is for God to decide, not us. We know that all of human history is in his hands. We needn't worry about that. We simply need to trust God to be as good as his word   to do good things for his children.

God's Glory in Answering Prayers

Speaking of human history leads to the third and final truth: God answers our prayers in order to demonstrate his might in the world and to vindicate his honor. You may recall that Israel lost a strategic battle at a city called Ai. Joshua, the leader, asked God that if the Jews turned their backs in defeat on their enemies, what would their enemies think of God (Josh. 7:9)? They would think that he was some puny little god. In Judges 6:13, Gideon appealed to God in much the same way: "If you really are Israel's God, what happened to all the promises you gave to us?"

God is vulnerable to our appeals to demonstrate his great power and vindicate his great honor in the earth because he desires to be praised and is worthy to be praised.

---

[4] Herbert Lockyer, *All the Prayers of the Bible*, 5.

So when we pray, we should ask God to exhibit his greatness in the earth. God desires and deserves worship and adoration. When we ask him to do great things, and he does them, he shows not just us, but the world, including the unbelieving world, how great he truly is. God did this with Pharaoh, he did it with Nebuchadnezzar, he did it with Nineveh, and he will do it today.

My mother was a godly, praying woman. A couple of years before she died, she submitted for her church's devotional manual an anecdote from our family history that I didn't know or else had forgotten:

> *"I will remember the works of the Lord: surely I will remember thy wonders of old" (Psalm 77:11).*

> There is something about recounting the mercies of God in the past that seems to fan again the flames of faith that have become embers of smoldering doubt in our prayer lives. Are there any among us, saved any amount of time, who have not seen the hand of God in our lives? I think this is why God tells us over and over in His Word to remember, to *"forget not all his benefits" (Psl. 103:2).*

> By God's grace, I will never forget the morning nearly fifty years ago when our firstborn, Andrew, looked at my husband and me, questioningly, when we told him he couldn't have any more cereal and milk, because there was no more — in fact, no more *anything.* Oh, and then the blessed memory of the knock that came at the back door just as the three of us were on our knees in the kitchen, praying for God to supply our need! A woman from church was standing there with bags of groceries in her hand that she said God had, for some reason, laid it upon her heart to bring to us. "Could you by any chance use them?" she asked, hesitantly. And, yes, there *was* cereal and milk in those bags!

Today, that little boy is a pastor, author, and much in demand as a preacher and conference speaker. And one of his favorite themes is — you guessed it— prayer.

> We will remember, we will remember;
> We will remember the works of your hand.
> We will shout and give you praise;
> For great is Thy faithfulness!

When we pray, let us pray bold, daring prayers, because those prayers honor God. Paltry, unbelieving prayers do not honor God, and it's therefore no wonder our age is marked by defeat, apostasy, and depravity.

> How futile is much of our wailing over our defeats and over the sick state of society around us! The first step to victory is to take up our weapons with the determination to go all out for victory.[5]

The first weapon is prayer, and prayer requires faith. Let us not forget the warning of Hebrews 3:12, "Beware, brethren, lest there be in any of you an evil heart of unbelief in departing from the living God." An unbelieving heart is an evil heart. An unbelieving heart leads us away from God. When we lack faith in God, including faith to answer our prayers, we begin to depart from the living God.

Conclusion

Let's review: (1) God isn't upset by big, daring prayers; he's upset by an evil heart of unbelief. (2) Don't worry about God's secret, eternal will when you pray; just act on what he's promised in his holy writing that's not-at-all-secret. (3) Always keep in mind that God loves to show his might and to vindicate his people in the world — so pray big prayers that will cause him to do that!

---

[5] R. Arthur Mathews, *Born for Battle* (Littleton, Colorado: OMF International, 2001), 60.

Let us pray bold, big, daring prayers, and expect God to act as he said he promised — and as he has acted so many times in the past. Pray big, expect big.

CHAPTER 3

DARE TO BE A DANIEL AT PRAYER

Introduction

You may have heard the Sunday school song, "Dare to be a Daniel." The chorus goes:

Dare to be a Daniel,
Dare to stand alone!
Dare to have a purpose firm!
Dare to make it known.

Daniel is one of the great, exemplary characters in the entire Bible. All of us are sinners, and have fallen short of God's glory, but that's not the fact that the Bible emphasizes (or even mentions[1]) in Daniel's life. Some people seem to have the idea that God reveals accounts of the Old Testament saints chiefly to highlight their sin and need for the coming Messiah. There's no doubt that they, and all

---

[1] Daniel acknowledges his own sin, but the Bible does not depict him as sinning

of us, need salvation in Jesus Christ, but "whatever things were written before [in the Old Testament] were written for our learning, that we through the patience and comfort of the Scriptures might have hope" (Rom. 15:4). The Old Testament examples are designed to give hope and faith to us who follow these saints. They are examples in how to live in faith and obedience before God.[2]

The Bible tells us specifically about Daniel to show us how a righteous man stands within an evil culture and hard circumstances. It reveals how God's sovereignty using one godly man works out in the life of a pagan culture to bring him glory.

Daniel was carried away with thousands of other Jewish youth to Babylon (modern Iran) in Judah's captivity. He and others were specifically selected to be the young elite in the Babylonian kingdom. Through a remarkable chain of providential circumstances, Daniel ended up as virtually the assistant to the king, Nebuchadnezzar and his royal successors. He was one of three governors directly under the king.

Just now I'll highlight one critical aspect of Daniel's high character: his prayer life. We don't live in a praying age. We don't live in a time in which families and churches and pastors and Christian children and college students spend much time in prayer. There's almost no preaching and teaching on prayer. Prayer is short, weak, and perfunctory.

As I noted before, Satan has a vested interest in cooling the ardor of Christians' prayer. He knows that prayer is God's chosen way of accomplishing much of his massive work in the earth, so Satan will do virtually anything to keep God's people from praying.

Obviously, in our time, he has been a rousing success.

---

[2] On the criticism that this approach is a wrongheaded "moralistic" interpretation, see John M. Frame, *The Escondido Theology* (Lakeland, Florida: Whitefield Theological Seminary, 2011), 47–52.

He wouldn't be a rousing success if more of us lived and prayed like Daniel. I'm invoking Daniel chapter 6:1–23, the account of Daniel's ordeal in the den of lions because of his sterling life of prayer:

> It pleased Darius to set over the kingdom one hundred and twenty satraps, to be over the whole kingdom; and over these, three governors, of whom Daniel [was] one, that the satraps might give account to them, so that the king would suffer no loss. Then this Daniel distinguished himself above the governors and satraps, because an excellent spirit [was] in him; and the king gave thought to setting him over the whole realm. So the governors and satraps sought to find [some] charge against Daniel concerning the kingdom; but they could find no charge or fault, because he [was] faithful; nor was there any error or fault found in him. Then these men said, "We shall not find any charge against this Daniel unless we find [it] against him concerning the law of his God." So these governors and satraps thronged before the king, and said thus to him: "King Darius, live forever! " All the governors of the kingdom, the administrators and satraps, the counselors and advisors, have consulted together to establish a royal statute and to make a firm decree, that whoever petitions any god or man for thirty days, except you, O king, shall be cast into the den of lions. "Now, O king, establish the decree and sign the writing, so that it cannot be changed, according to the law of the Medes and Persians, which does not alter." Therefore King Darius signed the written decree. Now when Daniel knew that the writing was signed, he went home. And in his upper room, with his windows open toward Jerusalem, he knelt down on his knees three times that day, and prayed and gave thanks before his God, as was his custom since early days. Then these men assembled and found Daniel praying and making supplication before his God. And they went before the king, and

spoke concerning the king's decree: "Have you not signed a decree that every man who petitions any god or man within thirty days, except you, O king, shall be cast into the den of lions?" The king answered and said, "The thing [is] true, according to the law of the Medes and Persians, which does not alter." So they answered and said before the king, "That Daniel, who is one of the captives from Judah, does not show due regard for you, O king, or for the decree that you have signed, but makes his petition three times a day." And the king, when he heard [these] words, was greatly displeased with himself, and set [his] heart on Daniel to deliver him; and he labored till the going down of the sun to deliver him. Then these men approached the king, and said to the king, "Know, O king, that [it is] the law of the Medes and Persians that no decree or statute which the king establishes may be changed." So the king gave the command, and they brought Daniel and cast [him] into the den of lions. [But] the king spoke, saying to Daniel, "Your God, whom you serve continually, He will deliver you." Then a stone was brought and laid on the mouth of the den, and the king sealed it with his own signet ring and with the signets of his lords, that the purpose concerning Daniel might not be changed. Now the king went to his palace and spent the night fasting; and no musicians were brought before him. Also his sleep went from him. Then the king arose very early in the morning and went in haste to the den of lions. And when he came to the den, he cried out with a lamenting voice to Daniel. The king spoke, saying to Daniel, "Daniel, servant of the living God, has your God, whom you serve continually, been able to deliver you from the lions?" Then Daniel said to the king, "O king, live forever! My God sent His angel and shut the lions' mouths, so that they have not hurt me, because I was found innocent before Him; and also, O king, I have done no wrong before you."

Now the king was exceedingly glad for him, and commanded that they should take Daniel up out of the den. So Daniel was taken up out of the den, and no injury whatever was found on him, because he believed in his God.

Note these exhortations.

Principled Prayer

First, dare to be a Daniel in *principled* prayer. Daniel's political colleagues (satraps, ancient Persian high politicians) were envious of him. They wanted to bring him down from his perch. Interestingly, they could find nothing in his work habits by which to accuse him. In other words, Daniel did his job, and he did it well. That, too, is an example for us. Christians of all people should be the most diligent and faithful in their work. What a smear on the name of Jesus Christ when professed Christians have shoddy work habits! That was not Daniel. He was not merely wise and loyal; he was diligent and provident.

So these satraps were forced to bring down Daniel in one way and one way alone: create a scenario in which his godly principles would conflict with his political status. Daniel had a well-deserved reputation for godliness:

> Then these men said, "We shall not find any charge against this Daniel unless we find it against him concerning the law of his God." (6:5)

The law of God

What a revival we need of the law of God! We live in a profoundly antinomian time. The law of God is neglected, perverted, belittled, slandered. Because they are aware that law isn't a means of our justification, many Christians throw it out the window. I would ask them to slowly read Psalm 119 and then consider whether they think themselves more spiritual than David. The law of God is a reflection of God's holy character, and he has called us to be holy. To attack the law of God is to attack the holiness of God. To attack the law of God is to attack the nature of God. To attack the law of God is to attack God. The Holy Spirit is given to us so that we can obey the law of God (Rom. 8:1–4). To be antinomian is to be anti-Christian.[3]

One command of the law of God is to pray. Daniel's pagan colleagues knew that this man was a man of prayer. He was a man of principled prayer. In other words, he formed the habits of prayer.

Romanticism and prayer

We live in a time drenched in the Romanticist notion that spontaneity is king. In the church, this means that godly habits and customs are sub-spiritual, while spontaneous, carefree, "Spirit-led" actions truly please God. Nothing could be further from the truth. The same Spirit who leads prophets to speak spontaneously leads them to spend time in prayer every day at the same time, and in the same way. Godly habits and customs aren't somehow less spiritual than godly spontaneity.

I urge you to set aside time, like Daniel, every day, to pray, to call out to God. Make a prayer list. There's nothing whatsoever sub-spiritual about a written prayer list. Unless your memory is superhuman, there's no way you can remember everyone and everything you need to pray for. It might not be necessary to pray through the entire list every day, but you probably need a list. In fact, if you can remember every person and everything you want to pray for every day, I suspect your prayer life is quite paltry. Your memory is not good enough to recall everyone and everything you need to pray for.

From a youth, Daniel had learned to pray (v. 10c). It was his custom. We'll never be people of prayer until prayer becomes a custom and habit. If we wait to pray until the exigencies of the

---

[3] P. Andrew Sandlin, *Public Christianity, Gospel and Law* (Coulterville, California: Center for Cultural Leadership, 2016), 22–31.

moment, we'll never be people of prayer. Prayer is a religious observance in the best sense. Jesus prayed at customary times. It's a principle of the Christian life. Every day we must acknowledge God as our Almighty and our Father. Every day we must glorify him in prayerful worship. Every day we must bring our requests to him. Every day we must show that we rely entirely on him for our life and provision. To go day after day without that kind of prayer — I'm not referring simply to hurried prayer over meals or public prayers at church — is to go day after day without any communion with the One in whom we live our very lives.

Religion with windows

Daniel refused to compromise his holy custom of prayer. Principles do not admit of compromise. Preferences can be compromised; principles can't. Daniel heard of Darius' foolish, idolatrous decree: that for thirty days no prayers could be made to any person or god except the king. The king loved Daniel, but Daniel's conniving colleagues persuaded Darius.

Notice what Daniel didn't say. He didn't say, "Well, I can pray silently, in my heart. A prayer in the heart is just as effective as a prayer out loud." No. Some of the old-timers were inclined to say, "Daniel's was religion with windows." He opened his windows like he did customarily and prayed to the Lord God.

It's astounding how timid and embarrassed Christians are about prayer, and they're not even facing a den of lions. When they're eating at a restaurant, they're too timid to pray aloud in a normal tone. They're too embarrassed to stop with a sinner or friend on the sidewalk or on an airplane and pray. I suspect they're actually ashamed of Jesus Christ. I suspect they don't want to be thought of as too religious. But we are religious. We're the people of God, and we rely on God in prayer, and the more an unbelieving culture knows this, the better. We don't pray to be seen of men, like the New Testament Pharisees did, but we also don't hide to avoid being seen by men — and consumed by lions.

Dare to be a Daniel in principled prayer.

Petitionary Prayer

Second, dare to be a Daniel in *petitionary* prayer. Chapter 9:1–19 consists almost entirely of Daniel's prayer for his people Israel. They were suffering so pitifully in Babylon. They deserved God's judgment for their sin, but he appeals to God to relieve his people:

> "Now therefore, our God, hear the prayer of Your servant, and his supplications, and for the Lord's sake cause Your face to shine on Your sanctuary, which is desolate." (9:17)

God invites us to come boldly in the name of Jesus Christ for help (Heb. 4:16). He delights to do good things for us.

False piety

One of the great errors of false prayer piety is the notion that it's self-centered to cry out to God to help us and give us good things. This idea is both perverse and counterproductive. When we pray, and when God answers our prayer, he does two things besides helping his people. First, God increases our faith and the faith of those people around us. We see what God does in answer to our prayer, and that increases our confidence that he will do even more.

In addition, as we noted in chapter 1, God displays his own glory in the earth by acting on behalf of his people. Note that after Daniel was delivered from the den of lions, King Darius issued a major proclamation honoring the Lord God (6:25–27). Answered prayer makes a deep impression not just on Christians, but also on nonbelievers. Answered prayer, therefore, helps to foster and undergird Christian culture.[4] Do you desire to glorify God? Then pray big prayers, and expect big answers.

---

[4] P. Andrew Sandlin, *Christian Culture: An Introduction* (Mount Hermon, California: Center for Cultural Leadership, 2013).

Asking God

God tells us that we don't have because we don't ask him (Jas. 4:2). If you need money for your family, ask God. If you desire a godly husband or wife, ask God. If you need physical healing, ask God. If you want your children or parents or your brother or sister or other relatives trust Jesus Christ, ask God. If you're having a problem with a friendship, cry out to God. If you need a seat on a plane that's fully booked, ask God. Don't assume that any request is too small. To say that a request is too small for God is to say that God isn't interested in every aspect of your life. That, of course, is nearly blasphemous doctrine.

Obviously, this truth implies that we should be praying all the time (1 Thes. 5:16): both customary prayer several times during the day, and scores or hundreds of short prayers throughout the day. If we understand that God wants to do good things for us and meet our needs throughout the day, then obviously we'll be in communion with God the entire day, because we have small needs throughout every day.

God is no sadist

I sometimes hear Christians imply or even state that God is committed to consistently testing and trying and bruising and hurting his children for his own glory, and that we should submit to this divinely inflicted injury. This is a slander and blasphemy. Jesus tells us that God is our Father, and that if we as sinful fathers love to do good things for children, how much more does our heavenly Father long to do good things for us his children who ask him (Mt. 7:9–11). I repeat the question: are you a better Father than God? Do you wish to harm and bruise and test your children? Then why in the world do you think God would want to do this? True, he does allow Satan to tempt us and hurl hardships in our way, but this is Satan's work, not God's.[5] In all things God is working for good in those of us who love him (Rom. 8:28).

---

[5] On the interplay between God's sovereignty and Satan's activity, see Michael S. Heiser, *The Unseen Realm* (Bellingham, Washington: Lexham, 2015), 61–67.

Daniel knew that God was not only a righteous God. He also knew that because God is a righteous God, he righteously loves and cares for his children. God sorrowfully sent his children into captivity because of their persistent sin, but he was more eager to forgive and restore them than he was to send them into captivity.

No prayer too little

I urge you to pray about everything. And by everything, I mean everything: church, family, friends, vocation, employment, family, money, fatigue, parking spaces, animals, allergies, phobias, gardens and grass and airplanes. If you think these are trivial, what you're really saying is that God isn't interested in the details of life. But the One who knows every sparrow that falls, and counts every hair on our heads, cares deeply for every aspect of our lives (Mt. 10:29–30). Therefore, pray about every dimension of your life. Pray about everything, and always.

Persevering Prayer

Finally, dare to be a Daniel in *persevering* prayer. We now meet Daniel as an old man (10:1–14). He's still praying. He's on his face before God. For twenty-one days he's been crying out for God to restore his people to Jerusalem and rebuild the temple. He's met on the banks of Tigris River by an angel in splendor and shining attire, so blazing in glory that the other Jews accompanying Daniel scampered away in fear. The angel made an arresting statement to Daniel. He wanted to assure Daniel that from the very first day that Daniel had begun fasting and praying, God had heard him and dispatched him (the angel) with the message. However, the angel had been impeded by the Prince of Persia on his way to bring the message.

There's little doubt about the meaning of the Prince of Persia. It's a fallen angel to whom Satan had given jurisdiction over the

Persian Empire.[6] By the way, we can learn from this that Satan has great interest in political rulers, and these demonic beings influence modern politicians for evil.[7]

For twenty-one days Daniel persevered in prayer. He didn't take the path of some of the falsely pious: "Well, I prayed for two long days, and God didn't answer; therefore, it must not be in his will." As I noted in chapter 2, it's not our responsibility to discover the will of God beyond the word of God. God's will for us to discover while on earth is set forth in his word. This is his prescriptive will. And one aspect of his prescriptive will is that we pray to our heavenly Father to meet our daily needs and answer our holy desires.

Daniel was a persevering prayer warrior, and God answered him because he persevered. God relishes persevering prayer. Jesus teaches:

> "Ask, and it will be given to you; seek, and you will find; knock, and it will be opened to you. For everyone who asks receives, and he who seeks finds, and to him who knocks it will be opened...." (Mt. 7:7–8)

From Daniel we know that many times our prayers aren't answered immediately because of great spiritual warfare in the heavens literally just above us. God has chosen not to annihilate Satan and his forces, but to get the victory for his people through great conflict over sin. Consider that fact for a moment, because it'll help you understand many things about God and Christianity and the Christian life. God chose not to annihilate sin but to defeat it. This means that he allows Satan and his hosts to continue their work. God refuses to give Satan the satisfaction of accomplishing his holy will by simply abolishing evil. God accomplishes this will by defeating evil through the instruments of his people and of his angels. This means that there're great battles that we must fight, and they're great battles

---

6 Heiser, 118–122.

7 Clinton E. Arnold, *Powers of Darkness* (Downers Grove, Illinois: InterVarsity, 1992), 202, 203.

of the heavenly realm, and many of those battles include angels arriving to answer our prayer after vanquishing Satanic adversaries.

Therefore, if you are praying, and praying for a long time, and your prayers aren't answered, don't stop praying. Don't assume what your prayer isn't in God's will. *Only rarely in the Bible does God reveal that the prayer of a godly person is not in his will* (Jas. 5:16). In the vast majority of cases, he answers the prayer of his righteous people, because righteous people pray righteous prayers.

The prayer worldview

Let me state as emphatically as possible: persevering prayer is an indispensable component of the Christian worldview. Ideas have consequences, but ideas alone won't change anything. We must have ideas that are fired with the power of the Holy Spirit in response to the prayers of God's people. To embrace the Christian worldview is to embrace the prayer worldview. If there's to be a great revival and reformation, it won't arrive only as a result of the power of ideas. They're necessary, but not sufficient. Those ideas must be backed up by principled, petitionary, and persevering prayer.

Conclusion

Let's not be filled with an evil heart of unbelief. Know that God is a good God who is eager to forgive sin, who longs to send great revival and reformation, who delights in the hearts of his children when they're delighted in him.

I conclude with the final two verses of the song "Dare to be a Daniel":

> Many giants, great and tall,
> Stalking through the land,
> Headlong to the earth would fall,
> If met by Daniel's band.
>
> Hold the Gospel banner high!

On to vict'ry grand!
Satan and his hosts defy,
And shout for Daniel's band.

CHAPTER 4

SOLA SCRIPTURA **PRAYER**

Introduction

One striking difference between our 18th and 19th century forebears and us is their repeated emphasis on prayer and our comparative de-emphasis of it. They prayed frequently and fervently. We pray infrequently and languidly. They called prayer meetings. We call staff meetings. They had revival and reformation. We have apathy and apostasy. A leading reason for these distinctions is that they were inclined to believe what God said about prayer. We are often less confident in God's word when it comes to his promises about prayer. A blunter way to say this is: we commit the sin of unbelief.

This is a severe indictment of conservative Protestants,

the group with which I identify, since we're formally committed to *sola Scriptura*, the Bible alone, a Reformation slogan. The best definition I ever encountered of *sola Scriptura* is John M. Frame's: "Scripture, and only Scripture, has the final word on everything . . . ."[1] We profess that if the Bible teaches it, that settles it, and we believe it. Too often, however, our lives belie our profession, and this is particularly the case with prayer. In this final chapter I'll communicate a few of our more prominent failures, some of which I touched on earlier.

God's Faithfulness In Not Answering Prayer?

The first is the popular inclination to defend God at all costs from the charge that he should have answered sincere prayers, but didn't. This is a righteous tendency. When God doesn't answer the requests of his children, he remains faithful. If we suppose that only when things are going well for us is God faithful, we implicitly endorse the false "prosperity gospel" and the "health-and-wealth gospel." God is faithful even when our life's circumstances are less than we desire, and even when God doesn't answer our prayers as swiftly as we'd prefer. God is faithful whether we consider him faithful or not.

But this perspective is one-sided, in that it often never gets around to considering another, and more important, truth; and because it does not, it leaves an incomplete impression. The truth is that God's faithfulness is dramatically verified by the answered prayers that improve our lot in life. The Bible is so clear and abundant about this truth of answered prayer that it is almost an embarrassment that one must document it. Here, I'll note only four texts from the Psalms:

> This poor man cried, and the LORD heard him and saved him out of all his troubles." (Ps. 34:6)

> Delight yourself in the Lord, and he will give you the desires of your heart. (Ps. 37:4)

---

[1] John M. Frame, *The Doctrine of the Word of God* (P & R Publishing: Phillipsburg, New Jersey, 2010), 571.

I love the LORD, because he has heard my voice and my pleas for mercy. (Ps. 116:1)

I thank you [God] that you have answered me and have become my salvation. (Ps. 118:21)

The New Testament is equally clear. God promises to answer the simple, heart-felt prayers of his children:

Again I say to you, that if two of you agree on earth about anything that they may ask, it shall be done for them by My Father who is in heaven. (Mt. 18:19)

Whatever you ask in My name, that will I do, so that the Father may be glorified in the Son. If you ask Me anything in My name, I will do it. (Jn. 14:13-14)

Truly, truly, I say to you, whatever you ask of the Father in my name, he will give it to you. Until now you have asked nothing in my name. Ask, and you will receive, that your joy may be full. (Jn. 16:23b–24)

Ask, and it will be given to you; seek, and you will find; knock, and it will be opened to you. For everyone who asks receives, and the one who seeks finds, and to the one who knocks it will be opened. Or which one of you, if his son asks him for bread, will give him a stone? Or if he asks for a fish, will give him a serpent? If you then, who are evil, know how to give good gifts to your children, how much more will your Father who is in heaven give good things to those who ask him! (Mt. 7:7-11)

The texts could be, and are, multiplied.[2] The Bible says or implies almost nothing about God's faithfulness in unanswered prayer, and he does not defend himself in the face of unanswered prayer. Why? Because the default is answered prayer for God's children. Struggle with the reality of unanswered prayer for obedient saints is not a great concern in the Bible, simply because God answers prayer.

Rationalizing a God Who Doesn't Answer Prayer

Too many Christians formally committed to *sola Scriptura*, however, are shy about these texts and others I could have cited, which means: they are shy about taking God at his word. They seem eager to defend God's honor in asserting that his faithfulness includes *not* answering our prayer. Heaven forbid we claim God is not faithful if he does not keep his word, in spite of the fact that this is just what the godly claimed in the Bible (Ex. 32:11–14; Jud. 6:1–18; 2 Chr. 20:1–12). They knew God's promises, and they expected him to fulfill his promises, and if he did not, they asserted he was not being faithful, and they told him so. This is why in Malachi 3:10 God charges a faithless and rebellious Israel, "Put me to the test," that is, trust me to prove to yourself whether my word is true. For us to scoff at this way of speaking to God, considering it sub-Christian, is simply rank unbelief decorated with a pious veneer. To refuse to hold God to his word is not a shining example of piety; it is a tragic example of faithlessness.

This biblical approach is too brazen for some Christians, however, particularly those most eager to defend God against the calumny that somebody prayed and God did not answer and, therefore, they were disappointed and have come to believe that God either isn't real or isn't a caring God. After all, our prayers these days are too often not answered, and this cannot be our fault due to our unbelief, despite the fact that this is just what Jesus taught (review again Mt. 6:30; 8:26; 16:8; Lk. 12:28). There must be some other explanation. For

---

[2] See Herbert Lockyer, *All the Prayers of the Bible* (Grand Rapids: Zondervan, 1959)

example, God has a secret, eternal, unrevealed, covert plan that contradicts his written word; and if we actually knew his hidden intentions, we could safely ignore his written promises that contradict them.[3] The fact that the Bible teaches that our unbelief can and does sometimes contribute to unanswered prayer is an unpleasant prospect that congregations don't like to hear, but the Bible does teach it (see also Mk. 6:1–6; 11:22–24; Jas. 1:6). E. M. Bounds wrote, "The millions of unanswered prayers are not to be solved by the mystery of God's will. We are not the sport of his sovereign power. He is not playing at 'make-believe' in his marvelous promises to answer prayer."[4]

Today unbelief is not a sin preachers are inclined to expose as nearly as preachers did in the past, despite the fact that unbelief is a damning sin, perhaps the most damning sin (Jn. 3:17–18). Instead we say that unanswered prayer is a result of God's covert purposes not disclosed in his written word, and in this way we contradict *sola Scriptura* while preserving our reputation of glorifying God. But God is not glorified when we blame our unbelief on his alleged covert purposes.

The "Triumph" of Unanswered Prayer?

The pastor of possibly the most noted historic evangelical church in the nation preached a message titled, "The Triumph of Unanswered Prayer."[5] No saint in the biblical record could have conceived of preaching or believing such a

---

[3] John Murray argues that God's eternally decreed will sometimes contradicts his declared desires. He concludes, "This is indeed mysterious." I would suggest it is so mysterious as to court incredulity. See *Collected Writings of John Murray* (Edinburgh: Banner of Truth, 1982), 4:131. God's revelatory actions do not contradict his eternal decrees. God is not double-minded or -tongued.

[4] E. M. Bounds, *The Complete Works of E. M. Bounds on Prayer* (Grand Rapids: Baker, 2004), 186.

[5] Erwin Lutzer (Moody Church, Chicago), "The Triumph of Unanswered Prayer," https://voice.dts.edu/chapel/the-triumph-of-unanswered-prayer-part-i-erwin-w-lutzer/, accessed January 24, 2018.

thing. The pastor is properly concerned with those Christians who lose faith because they have suffered great loss or pain and illness and have not gotten their prayers answered, and have resolved never to pray again. The pastor's intentions are pure, but his construction is wrong. The Bible nowhere teaches that the Christian should rejoice when God does not answer prayer. If God does not answer prayer, the Bible often supplies other explanations than his covert intentions that contradict the promises of his word: unbelief (Jas. 1:6–8), inward iniquity (Ps. 66:18), despising God's law (Pr. 28:9), self-indulgence (Jas. 4:3), and Satanic interference (Dan. 10). Conflict with God's covert, unrevealed desires is not given as an explanation for unanswered prayer.

"Unanswered prayers," declares E. M. Bounds, "are training schools for unbelief."[6] On the other hand, answered prayer is a ringing apologetic for the glory and power of God:

> Never did the church need more than now those who can raise up everywhere memorials of God's supernatural power, memorials of answers to prayer, memorials of promises fulfilled. These would do more to silence the enemy of souls, the foe of God and the adversary of the church than any modern scheme or present day plan for the success of the gospel. Such memorials reared by praying people would dumbfound God's foes, strengthen weak saints, and would fill strong saints with triumphant rapture.[7]

The "Internal Benefit Thesis"

In addition, a spurious distraction from the biblical promises of answered prayer mentioned earlier is the frequent suggestion that the great benefit of prayer is that it changes the petitioner. Prayer directs our attention to God, instills holy habits, and crowds out worldly desires. We might call this the

---

[6] E. M. Bounds, *The Complete Works of E. M. Bounds on Prayer*, 187.
[7] Bounds, 108.

"internal benefit thesis" of prayer. No doubt prayer does create virtue and holiness in the pray-er, but that fact is almost never mentioned in the Bible. E. Bounds dismisses this thesis with a flourish:

> We have much fine writing and learned talk about the subjective benefits of prayer; how prayer secures its full measure of results, not by affecting God, but by affecting us, by becoming a training school for those who pray. We are taught by such teachers that the province of prayer is not to get, but to train. Prayer thus becomes a mere performance, a drill-sergeant, a school, in which patience, tranquility and dependence are taught. In this school, denial of prayer is the most valuable teacher. How well all this may look, and how reasonable soever it may seem, there is nothing of it in the Bible. The clear and oftrepeated language of the Bible is that prayer is to be answered by God; that God occupies the relation of a father to us, and that as Father He gives to us when we ask the things for which we ask. The best praying, therefore, is the praying that gets an answer.[8]

The "internal benefit thesis" is suitable to a self-centered age that prizes subjectivism. Ironically, some of the very same people that (rightly) abhor the "prosperity gospel" as reflecting self-centered prayer embrace the "internal benefit thesis," which deemphasizes prayer that boldly implores God to change the status quo in the world so that many will see his power and glorify him, and redirects it toward personal spiritual growth. The Bible implies that prayer does enhance our sanctification and spiritual growth, by this is not the chief benefit of prayer. Prayer changes the status quo; it usually glorifies God in a very empirical, verifiable, public way.

---

[8] Bounds, 230.

The New "Liberal Evangelicals" At Prayer

Many of the same conservative Protestants who castigate their benighted evangelical and Pentecostal brothers and sisters or "liberal evangelicals" for adjusting the Bible to their own experience apparently have no problem adjusting the Bible to their own experience when it means suggesting that they lack faith in God's promises to answer the simple, heart-felt requests of his people. They explain away passages that unambiguously promise that God will answer the faith-filled prayers of his people. Since the Bible plainly teaches that homosexuality is sin, they correctly rebuke those "liberal evangelicals" who twist the Bible into saying what it plainly does not. But when it comes to biblical promises about answered prayer, they adopt the skeptical methodology of the very people they criticize; they believe the Bible only when it conforms to their experiences. The "Bible alone" rules — except when we find biblical promises about prayer inconvenient.

Christian Antisupernaturalism

This is one aspect of the creeping antisupernaturalism that afflicts the orthodox, though we would be the last to admit that Enlightenment antisupernaturalism has impacted our thinking (that problem is for liberals, not us). We are quite certain that God exists and that he upholds the world and that he regenerates believing sinners. But we are less audacious when it comes to God's interference in creation in response to our crying out to him in prayer. "[T]he biblical writers and those to whom they wrote were predisposed to supernaturalism."[9] By contrast, we are predisposed to naturalism. Our default is to appeal to antisupernatural explanations of events in history and our lives unless a supernatural explanation alone will suffice. This is to reverse the biblical order.

---

[9] Michael S. Heiser, *The Unseen Realm* (Bellingham, Washington: Lexham Books), 19

The antisupernaturalist Christians know that the Bible does not promise that God will answer every possible faith-filled prayer of his people, and they point as verification of this thesis to (1) David's prayer for his child with Bathsheba, (2) Jesus' prayer in Gethsemane, and (3) Paul's prayer for the removal of the "thorn" of his flesh. They are quite right. What they often fail to assert is that these are likely the only examples in the Bible of clearly unanswered prayers by the godly.[10] When we read the Bible, we arrive at some arresting statistics, as I pointed out in chapter 2. Even apart from the Psalms, which are full of prayers, "[T]he Bible records no fewer than 650 definite prayers, of which no less than 450 have recorded answers."[11] That's a noteworthy proportion of answered prayers.

Righteousness Versus the "Prosperity Gospel"

The reluctance to embrace such audacity is driven partly by aversion to the "prosperity gospel" or "health-and-wealth gospel," according to which God exists to glut his children with all of life's lustful bounty that their carnal minds desire. But the Bible is quite clear that such an approach is wrong. God does not answer prayer to satiate our own lusts (Jas. 4:3). More significantly, we learn from James 5:16 that it is the effectual prayer of righteous persons that obtains answers in heaven's court. Righteous people pray righteous prayers. God is not interested in the prayers of lust-drenched, narcissistic people. The biblical promises of answered prayer are directed to Christians who wish above all things to please God.

Prayer and Predestination

Next, consider the apparent tension between prayer and

---

[10] E. M. Bounds, *The Complete Works of E. M. Bounds on Prayer*, 197.
[11] Herbert Lockyer, *All the Prayers of the Bible*, 5.

predestination.[12] I counseled in each of the three previous chapters that we should pray according to the prescriptive will of God (in the Bible) and not the decretal will of God (in his secret counsels). The decrees of God come to the forefront in predestination. The Bible is a predestinarian book (Pr. 16:4; Ac. 2:23–24, 4:27–28; Rom. 8:30; Eph. 1:5, 11). Literally, predestination means to determine a destiny beforehand. Predestination is that aspect of the decrees or secret counsel of God that more specifically pertains the humanity: what God has determined beforehand for humanity and specific individuals. The Bible teaches that God predestines man and woman. However, the Bible is less interested in disclosing how that predestination works itself out in human history.

In Exodus we read that God hardened Pharaoh's heart to accomplish his purposes with his people Israel, but this explanation is an exception. God generally accomplishes his secret will with mankind without telling us how he does this. Prayer itself, however, is an obvious means of fulfilling his plan, and how he uses prayer doesn't always conform to easy cause-and-effect theories of predestination. For example, we know that Jesus Christ is the Lamb slain from the world's foundation (Rev. 13:7), a supreme event determined by God's will (Ac. 2:23–24). However, to Peter, drawing his sword to protect Jesus from capture in the Garden of Gethsemane, Jesus asks rhetorically, "Or do you think that I cannot now pray to My Father, and He will provide Me with more than twelve legions of angels?" It won't suffice to say this could never have happened when Jesus plainly says it could have. Jesus states that prayer could have averted the Cross (Mt. 26:53)! He goes on to say (v. 54) that he did not pray for deliverance precisely because he wanted the Scriptures fulfilled. In other words, he chose to fulfill the Scriptures, but prayer could have averted God's stated plan — even of the crucifixion. We know that in the Garden Jesus prayed that he could avoid the cup of his impending, atoning death, despite the fact that he knew this world-saving death was in Father's will. We cannot say that our Lord was

---

[12] For a thoughtful treatment, see Roger T. Forster and V. Paul Marston, *God's Strategy in Human History* (Minneapolis: Highland Books, 1973).

ignorant of that will, so we must acknowledge that he was praying for God to change his will, though he finally surrendered to that divine will. These Scriptures alone should caution us to avoid undue certainty in defining the decrees of God and predestination.[13]

John writes, "Now this is the confidence that we have in Him, that if we ask anything according to His will, He hears us" (1 Jn. 5:14). Some people assume that by "will of God" John denotes the eternal decrees of God. The meaning then would be that God answers us if we pray according to what his secret counsels have appointed. This interpretation is not self-evident. The context (v. 16) mentions prayer for one who has grievously sinned, and God promises that if we pray for him, God will deliver him. This hardly sounds like John is thinking about God's eternal decrees. He's denoting the prescriptive will of God. Matthew Henry's commentary on this verse is warranted, then, in suggesting:

> The Lord Christ emboldens us to come to God in all circumstances, with all our supplications and requests. Through him our petitions are admitted and accepted of God. The matter of our prayer must be agreeable to the *declared will of God*. It is not fit that we should ask what is contrary either to his majesty and glory or to our own good, who are his and dependent on him. And then we may have confidence that the prayer of faith shall be heard in heaven. [14]

Perhaps what we call the decrees of God are not as inflexible as we sometimes believe, or perhaps we should

---

[13] Bruce Ware exhibits this inflexibility in "Prayer and the Sovereignty of God," *For the Fame of God's Name*, Sam Storms and Justin Taylor, eds. (Wheaton, Illinois: Crossway, 2010), 126–143.

[14] Matthew Henry, *Commentary on the Whole Bible*, at 1 John 5, https://www.blueletterbible.org/Comm/mhc/1Jo/1Jo_005.cfm?a=1164014, accessed January 30, 2018, emphasis supplied.

modify our definition of God's decrees and predestination.[15]

Impatient, predestination-obsessed petitioners

It is this belief that God's will is set in stone that generates such timidity and impatience in prayer. How often we pray, and if God doesn't answer in a month (or week or day or year), we respond, "Well, it must not have been in his will." To my knowledge, no one in the Bible reasoned this way, and Paul quit praying to be delivered from his famous fleshly thorn only when God specifically revealed to him his will. Abraham (Gen. 18:32), Jacob (Gen. 32:26), Moses (Dt. 9:18), Elijah (Jas. 5:17), the Syrophoenician woman (Mt. 15:27), the Capernaum nobleman (Jn. 4:49), and the Jerusalem church (Ac. 12:5) persevered in prayer and did not cease with the excuse that their request was apparently not in God's predestined will. P. T. Forsyth assails this attitude:

> There are many plain obstacles to the deepening of spiritual life, amid which I desire to name here only one; it is prayer conceived merely, or chiefly, as submission, resignation, quietism. We say too soon, "Thy will be done"; and too ready acceptance of a situation as His will often means feebleness or sloth. It may be His will that we surmount His will. It may be His higher will that we resist His lower. Prayer is an act of will much more than of sentiment, and its triumph is more than acquiescence. Let us submit when we must, but let us keep the submission in reserve rather than in action, as a ground tone rather than the stole effort. Prayer with us has largely ceased to be wrestling. But is that not the dominant scriptural idea? It is not the sole idea, but is it not the dominant? And is not our subdued note often

---

15 E. M. Bounds, *The Complete Works of E. M. Bounds on Prayer*, 276, 277.

but superinduced and unreal?[16]

The Bible never counsels the cessation of our prayers on the grounds that the answer conflicts with his secret counsels. If anything, he seems disposed to change his declared course of action if the godly persevere in prayer. God's will includes a desire that we wrestle with his stated purposes. P. T. Forsyth again:

> When we resist the will of God we may be resisting what God wills to be temporary and to be resisted, what He wills to be intermediary and transcended. We resist because God wills we should. We are not limiting God's will, any more than our moral freedom limits it. That freedom is the image of His, and, in a sense, part of His. We should defraud Him and His freedom if we did not exercise ours. So the prayer which resists His dealing may be part of His will and its fulfilment.[17]

We do not limit God's will when we resist his (apparent) will. We should be much less concerned with God's eternal decrees than with his inscripturated promises to answer those who persevere in faith.

Where Classical Theism Violates *Sola Scriptura*

Finally, at the root of much Christian skepticism about prayer is an imbalanced view of God that developed early in the church under the influence of Greek philosophy.[18] The Greeks believed that emotion and changeableness were inferior

---

[16] P. T. Forsyth, *The Soul of Prayer*, https://www.ccel.org/ccel/forsyth/prayer/files/soul_of_prayer09.htm, accessed February 1, 2018.

[17] Forsyth, https://www.ccel.org/ccel/forsyth/prayer/files/soul_of_prayer09.htm.

[18] Edwin Hatch, *The Influence of Greek Ideas on Christianity* (New York, Harper & Brothers, 1957), 116–138.

qualities. Therefore, the highest deity they could think of was a god who had no emotions and who never changed his mind. The problem is that this isn't a person. A person has emotions and changes his mind. Emotion is not sin. Changing your mind is not sin. You're not somehow inferior because you have emotions or change your mind. And since God is the greatest possible person, he has emotions, and he changes his mind. In classical theism, however, God is unchanging (immutable) and unemotional (impassible) in ways that he cannot be moved (emotionally, and to action) by our prayers.[19] I noted in chapter 1 specific biblical texts stating that God does in fact change his mind toward man.[20] While God is in fact unchanging in his qualities and character, he is not unchanging in his relation to mankind, despite what classical theism has taught.[21] A better term than immutability might be "constancy"; "[T]he biblical view is not that God is static but stable."[22] If we argue that God is immutable in a sense different from and beyond his unvarying stability, constancy and dependability, we envision a god different from the biblical God. The Bible alone defines who God is and what he is like. In this vein, J. I. Packer warns of the "mystification of God":

> By "mystification" I mean the idea [of classical theism] that some biblical statements about God

---

[19] Unfortunately, on this point, classical theism's view of God bears an uncomfortable resemblance to the ancient Gnostic view of the greatest god, sitting atop the hierarchy of divine beings. See Benjamin Walker, *Gnosticism, Its History and Influence* (Wellingborough, England: Aquarian Press, 1983), 28–32.

[20] For theological and philosophical criticisms of immutability and impassibility in classical theism, see Thomas V. Morris, "God and the World," *Process Theology*, Ronald H. Nash, ed. (Grand Rapids: Baker Book House, 1987), 281–306.

[21] "[W]e must not confuse the philosophical thought of God as the epitome of minimal conditions of talk about him with the actual reality of God. This concept is not identical with the essence of God which reveals itself in his historical acts," Wolfhart Pannenberg, *Systematic Theology* (Grand Rapids: Eerdmans, 1988), 1:394. This is a noteworthy admission from a theologian deeply committed to philosophical theology.

[22] Millard Erickson, *Christian Theology* (Grand Rapids: Baker, 1985), 1:278–279.

mislead as they stand, and ought to be explained away....

[S]ometimes [in the Bible] God is said to change his mind and to make new decisions as he reacts to human doings. Orthodox theists have insisted that God does not *really* change his mind since God is impassible and never a "victim" of his creation. As writes Louis Berkhof, representative of this view, "the change is not in God, but in man and man's relations to God."

But to say that is to say that some things that Scripture affirms about God do not mean what they seem to mean, and do mean what they do not seem to mean. This provokes the question: How can these statements be part of the *revelation* of God when they actually *misrepresent and so conceal* God? In other words, how may we explain these statements about God's grief and repentance without seeming to explain them away?

[A]t every point in his self-disclosure God reveals what he essentially is, with no gestures that mystify. And surely we must reject as intolerable any suggestion that God *in reality* is different at any point from what Scripture makes him appear to be. Scripture was not written to mystify and therefore we need to ask how we can dispel the contrary impression that the time-honored, orthodox line of explanation leaves.[23]

This flexibility in his relationship with man isn't an indication of a God who is less than sovereign; rather, an emotionless God who cannot be touched by our prayers and

---

[23] J. I. Packer, "What Do You Mean When You Say God?" *Christianity Today*, September 19, 1986, 30, emphases in original.

infirmities is less than a person.[24] The fact that he cannot be surprised or overwhelmed by our prayers (or sins) does not mean that he lacks emotion or is unchanging in every sense. God, of his sovereign choice, experiences change and emotions as only the Creator can, but he does experience them.[25] To say that he cannot is to mystify God — and depict him as having (or lacking) traits not in harmony with the Bible's depiction of him. Donald G. Bloesch is correct, therefore, that "[P]etitionary prayer is logically undercut by classical theists."[26] In response to our prayers, God is eager to change his declared course of actions, though man can never finally thwart God's purposes (Job 42:2; Prov. 19:21; Is. 14:27).

The default assumption of Christians is that God will answer their prayers. To shy away from this truth is to bear an evil heart of unbelief (Heb. 3:12).

Conclusion

In 1915 Moody Press published a book by Charles Blanchard, the second president of Wheaton College, arguably the most prominent evangelical college in the country (both then and now). The full title was *Getting Things from God: Great Chapters on Prayer*. A chief theme of the book is that answered prayer means getting from God precisely what we pray for. He abhorred the prevalent idea (both then and now) that "no" from God is an answer to prayer. Answered prayer, according to Blanchard, denotes that God gives his children what they ask

---

[24] Ronald H. Nash, *The Concept of God* (Grand Rapids: Zondervan, 1983), 99–105.

[25] John M. Frame, *The Doctrine of God* (Phillipsburg, New Jersey: P & R Publishing, 2002), 558.

[26] Donald G. Bloesch, *God the Almighty* (Downers Grove: InterVarsity, 1995), 256. Classical theists are understandably on guard against the modern trend to adjust God to man's ideas and desires such as we find in process theology and open theism, which are heretical views of God. Our objective, however, must be grasping and understanding biblical truth, not staking out the ground at the greatest distance from heresy. The Bible must rule. Refuting process theology, see Carl F. H. Henry, *God, Revelation and Authority* (Waco, Texas: Word, 1983), 6:52–75, and on open theism, see John M. Frame, *No Other God* (Phillipsburg, New Jersey: P & R Publishing, 2001)

him for. It is almost inconceivable that any evangelical college president today would write a book with this audacious, faith-drenched title and argument. Reviving prayer as a mighty force in the church and culture is simply not high on the evangelical agenda. And then we puzzle over the paltry influence of Christianity in church and culture.

But the Bible everywhere expects God's people to expect God to do just what he says he will do — including, perhaps especially, to answer the prayer of his righteous, faith-filled people. It also declares that God will not answer the prayers of those who do not expect him to work — in other words, unbelieving, doubtful people cannot expect God to answer their paltry, unbelieving prayers:

> If any of you lacks wisdom, let him ask of God, who gives to all liberally and without reproach, and it will be given to him. But let him *ask in faith, with no doubting,* for *he who doubts is like a wave of the sea driven and tossed by the wind.* For let not that man suppose *that he will receive anything from the Lord;* he is a double-minded man, unstable in all his ways. (Jas. 1:5-8, emphasis supplied)

Protestant reformer John Calvin, whose emphasis on predestination some might assume would set him at odds with an equally strong emphasis on confidence in prayer, writes:

> What kind of prayer would this be? "O Lord, I am indeed doubtful whether or not thou art inclined to hear me; but being oppressed with anxiety I fly to thee that if I am worthy, thou mayest assist me." *None of the saints whose prayers are given in Scripture thus supplicated.* Nor are we thus taught by the Holy Spirit, who tells us to "come boldly unto the throne of grace, that we may obtain mercy, and find grace to help in time of need," (Heb. 4:16); and elsewhere teaches us to "have boldness and access with

confidence by the faith of Christ," (Eph. 3:12). This confidence of obtaining what we ask, a confidence which the Lord commands, and all the saints teach by their example, we must therefore hold fast with both hands, if we would pray to any advantage. *The only prayer acceptable to God is that which springs (if I may so express it) from this presumption of faith, and is founded on the full assurance of hope.*[27]

If the Bible is true, then we can expect that when with simple, honest, obedient faith we cry out to God for material provision, he will supply it. When we beg God to heal the sick, he will heal them. When we implore God to convert our unbelieving friends and relatives, he will convert them. When we pray and fast for God to send revival in the church and reformation the culture, that's just what we will see. And if we do not receive these answers, we should persevere in prayer, and we should not warp the Bible to conform to our paltry experiences but ask whether we have not met the conditions God lays down for answering prayer.

Four things let us ever keep in mind: God hears prayer, God heeds prayer, God answers prayer, and God delivers by prayer. These things cannot be too often repeated. Prayer breaks all bars, dissolves all chains, opens all prisons and widens all straits by which God's saints have been holden.[28]

We do not really believe the Bible if we do not believe God's promises to answer prayer.

---

[27] John Calvin, *Institutes of the Christian Religion*, Bk. 3, Ch. 20, Sec. 7, http://www.biblestudytools.com/history/calvin-institutes-christianity/book3/chapter-20.html, accessed November 21, 2016, emphases supplied.

[28] E. M. Bounds, *The Complete Works of E. M. Bounds on Prayer*, 522.

ABOUT THE AUTHOR

P. Andrew Sandlin is Founder and President of the Center for Cultural Leadership. He is a cultural theologian and an ordained Gospel minister in the Fellowship of Mere Christianity. He is faculty at the Blackstone Legal Fellowship, Edinburgh Theological Seminary, Evan Runner International Academy of Cultural Leadership, and the Wilberforce Academy. He and his wife Sharon have five adult children and three grandchildren.

Made in the USA
Monee, IL
24 February 2020